True Fables
Stories from Childhood

by
Catherine Ann Jones

Published by Prasana Press

105 S. Arnaz Ave, Ojai, CA 93023 USA

www.wayofstory.com

catherinejones@wayofstory.com

ISBN 978-0-9765352-3-2 (paperback)

True Fables: Stories from Childhood by Catherine Ann Jones

Book Layout by Mayo Morley

Acknowledgment of Margaret Keane's painting, *Waiting*

1. Children age four and up, 2. memoir, 3. fables

For Grant and Erika

and

their wonder-full children, Gracen, Aria, & Gion

෴

Table of Contents

Author's Note

It is a still stranger thing that there is nothing
so delightful in the world as telling stories.

Virginia Woolf

A therapist friend challenged me to write children's stories taken
from my own childhood memories. He further invited me to
come every so often and share these stories with his three young

children. So, thinking 'I've never done that before so this sounds like fun', I accepted the challenge. Every two weeks, I would write a new story then drive over to my friend's wife and three children (the therapist being at work) for Story Hour.

We've had fifteen stories so far and the children won't let me stop. Though pre-school age, the children sit and listen to the short stories, many which involve former pets and adventures from my childhood, a horse born on my birthday, a black lamb given me on Easter, two ducklings won at the State

Fair, living in Japan, and others. Then we all take paper and crayons or colored pencils and draw the story. This is my Green Dragon that came from one of the stories called *Cloud People.*

The oldest child, a lively boy, suggested we all become the animals. So now after the story and the drawing, we become the story. We play. Remember play? I had largely forgotten how important play is at any age. And surprisingly, when we join the very young at play, that very young person we once were comes alive again. Isn't that great?

So, it is my deep wish that all who read or listen to these *True Fables*, also draw and play them. And, maybe, just maybe, be inspired to make up your own stories.

Catherine Ann Jones
Ojai, California

A Train for Christmas

O ne Christmas I was hoping and wishing for a train. I thought about trains, I dreamed about trains, all I could think about was trains. I must have been very, very good that year because come Christmas morning, I woke up and there was a big box that said Toy Electric Train. Well, I couldn't wait for breakfast so I tore into the big box and started unwrapping each bright red car. First the locomotive which drove the train, then two passenger cars where the people who were going somewhere sat and looked out the windows, and finally the caboose which was the end car of the train.

Then I had to unwrap the train tracks and the operator

box where the operator - that's me - would make the train go and stop, slow or fast. It took quite a while to put it all together but Mother and Grandfather helped me. Gram was in the kitchen making Christmas breakfast of waffles and strawberries. The smell was so good that we all decided to take a break and have Christmas breakfast downstairs. What could be better on Christmas morning than hot waffles, lots of butter and maple syrup, topped with strawberries? Yummy! Still, I didn't take long to eat as I had a train to put together and tracks to lay down and a cord to plug in, so that I could operate my very own train.

Finally, the tracks were laid in a big circle so that the train could go around and round, the train was hitched up, all the cars in a row, and the operator's box was plugged in and waiting. I called out "All aboard!" then pulled the switch ever so slowly to make sure the train stayed on the track. Luckily, it did as it began to move. All was well so I pushed the switch to go faster and faster and faster. What fun! Then, uh-oh, as my fast train was coming around a curve on the track at the top of the circle, guess what happened? One of the cars fell off the track, and because all the cars were connected, the whole train fell off the track. Crash! Boom! Oh, dear. I rushed to put it right. I had learned something important for a train operator. That is, when the train is coming where the track bends in a circle, you have to slow down so there are no accidents. I was more careful next time and guess what? There were no more accidents.

Next, I learned that the locomotive could make a sound and steam would come out, like a real old steam engine. How cool is that!

Later my mother told me there was another gift under the tree that I'd want to see right away. So, I skipped downstairs fast as lightning, wondering whatever could it be. I only asked for an electric train and it was already here. Well, under the Christmas tree, there was another big box with my name on it. So, I opened the bright red wrapping and saw that it was a cowboy town like in the old wild west days. This would go in the center so the train would go around the town. Wow. That's really neat.

So, the whole rest of the morning, I began to create the old western town in the middle of the train tracks. There were buildings and people and horses. Then when it looked like a real live old western town, I just watched it and got another idea.

Here was a new town with cowboys and women and boys and girls, dogs, horses, a bank, a school, a church, a hotel and so on. Something was missing. What could it be? I sat quiet and didn't move until I knew what was missing.

Can you guess what it was?

A story! A town was a place where stories happen. So, we must make up a good story with the people and horses and dogs and things.

It was in the wild, wild west almost two hundred years ago in America and the town was new. People had come from far away to live in the west and raise their families. But there was also danger like outlaws so they needed someone to be the sheriff of the town to make sure that everyone was safe. Let's ask Tom to be the sheriff. Then the cowboy dressed in black would be the outlaw who tries to rob the bank and take everyone's money. And then …

❖ Will he succeed?

❖ What happens next?

Two Ducklings and
the Texas State Fair

T here are county fairs all over the country and they are quite nice of course, but nothing compares to the Texas State Fair. Largest in America. Huge – and great fun, too. I was maybe ten or eleven. It was Oct so I was off to the Fair. The exhibits in different buildings were quite interesting and varied, from the Hope Diamond – the world's largest diamond - to how people lived in Africa or Egypt or

Mexico and the beautiful objects they made. Blankets, ceramic dishes, jewelry, toys and dolls. One year I entered my own doll collection and won the Blue Ribbon – that's first place in all of Texas. My dolls came from all over the world and I would take them out of the tall glass cabinet where they lived, and make up stories about who they were and what lives they led. But this isn't the story I meant to tell you today.

Today I will tell you about the games one played at the Texas State Fair and, if very, very lucky, the prizes one could win there. The year before I won a tall beautiful doll because I threw a ball in the hoop three times. This year was different. It was different because I won a living, walking, noisy something. Can you guess what that was? And I didn't just win one but I won two. First, let me tell you how I won this special prize. .There were small bowls set far from where you had to stand and you had to throw coins and hope to land the coins inside the bowls. First, I looked at the tiny bowls far away and thought about how best to throw the coins. Then I took a deep breath and holding a quarter in my hand and keeping an eye on the bowl, I took aim and threw the coin. Clunk. It landed square in the bowl. Instead of taking a little prize, I decided to toss again and again. Clunk. Clunk. This made three times that the coin landed in the bowls.

Then the fellow who ran the stand, pointed to what my prize was. A little cage with two yellow baby ducklings. Real live baby ducks! I gave him a big smile and laughed out loud. "You mean I can take those baby ducks home?" "Yep, you sure can. They're yours." Wow.

This began my life with two yellow baby ducklings. I called them Fanny and Freddie. One behind the other, they followed me around, everywhere. Waddle. Waddle.

And when I would lay down on the grass, you know what? Those baby ducks would climb all over me, going Quack! Quack! all the while.

❖ Can you sound like a duck?

❖ Can you waddle like a duck?

Danny, a Black Lamb

M y mother and I lived with my grandparents in Texas. Each and every year at Easter, they surprised me with an Easter gift. This was no ordinary Easter present. This was something living.

One year it was a white bunny, another year fifty colored baby chicks. This year I stayed awake wondering what live creature would be there on Easter morning. Imagine my surprise when I quickly showered and dressed and ran downstairs then outside to see what I least expected to see!

There on the grass just in front of our home was a small

black lamb. As soon as we saw each other, the lamb said, "Ba-a-a" and I knew he was meant for me. Earlier I had read a story about a little boy who lived with his grandmother in the woods somewhere, on a farm, and they were very, very poor. The boy, Jeremiah, dreamed of having a champion horse to win a blue ribbon at the county fair. But, being very, very poor, there was no way he could afford to buy such a horse – or indeed any horse at all. Then someone gave him a black lamb and at first, he made fun of it. A lamb maybe, but lambs are white and become fluffy white sheep and they sometimes might win a blue ribbon at the county fair, but a black lamb, never!

Then that night Jeremiah had a dream. In the dream, a wise old owl danced around his head singing, "You've got to do with what you got." Jeremiah woke up the next morning and understood that that wise old owl was trying to tell him something. And that something was if someone gives you a black lamb, well, you've got to do with that because that's what you have.

So, Jeremiah worked hard to raise and care for the black lamb. He named the lamb, Danny, and though it wasn't easy, there came the day of the county fair and Jeremiah took his lamb to the fair. People laughed at someone entering a black lamb when all the other lambs were white and worth so much more. The judges chose a white lamb for the blue ribbon and Jeremiah was crushed, but tried not to show how unhappy and disappointed he was. You see, in his young mind, Danny was like no other lamb, but was every bit a champion, too. His grandmother said to Danny, "Never mind, boy, let's go home." And Danny looked up at him and said, "Ba-a-a". Jeremiah untied the rope and turning his back on the judges and all the people there started home. "Wait. Wait there, young man." Jeremiah turned back around and saw the old judge waving at him to come back into the arena. Why was this? wondered Jeremiah, but he and Danny walked back. Then the old judge said to everyone. "We felt that this year an exception should be made and a special ribbon given to something we've never seen before. Never has anyone entered a black lamb into this competition at the fair. And the love and care given to this little black lamb shows that as far as black lambs are, this is probably a champion all its own. So, ladies and gentlemen, this year, the fair is giving a special blue ribbon to Jeremiah Kinkaid and his black lamb. The crowd who was a few moments ago laughing at them, started to clap and cheer. Jeremiah saw his grandmother's face light up then waving him to go up and accept their prize. Danny said, "Ba-a-a." And the boy and his black lamb proudly walked up on the stage to the judges and was given a special blue ribbon. This was a day Jeremiah would never ever forget and inside his mind, he thanked that wise old owl for telling him "You got to do with what you got."

So, that Easter when I saw this black lamb, my very own black lamb, that's why I named him Danny.

❖ What is something you have that you have to 'do with what you got'?

Mr. Lucky

Being a Texas girl and a tomboy, my dream was to have a horse of my very own. I had learned to ride on my Uncle Grady's farm a few miles away and collected those plastic horses that girls sometimes collect. I read countless horse stories such as Black Beauty, Thunderhead, Flicka, and others. I used to sit on my grandparents' bed post imagining it was a real horse and ride and ride until one day I broke the bed post and was told not to do that anymore. Finally, at age eleven, I came home one day from school and my grandfather took me outside and introduced me to Babe, a large white mare that was to be mine.

I immediately climbed up on her, felt the hard saddle under me, took the reins, and rode. All too soon, Babe bucked and threw me into a cactus patch. The cactus needles stung like blazes. Even so, my grandfather offered no sympathy. He told me that if I didn't climb back up then and there, the horse would always remember that. So, I did climb back on, and you know what? That horse never threw me again. Good lesson for life! (My grandmother later used tweezers and helped pick out the cacti needles.)

Later, Babe gave birth to Mr. Lucky, so named as he was born on Friday the 13th in April, which just happened to be my birthday! He was sired by Barracuda, a prize thoroughbred from the King Ranch, the largest ranch in Texas. It was love at first sight. Lucky was a chestnut sorrel with a narrow white streak on his face, and three white socks. As any other proud parent, I stopped at the 7-11 store on the way to school that Friday and purchased pink bubble gum cigars to hand out to the kids at school. From age twelve to eighteen, Lucky was my main love.

Boys came much later. We played together, Mr. Lucky and me. One game was hike and seek. I would tell him to stay then I would run away somewhere and hide behind a bush. Then I whistled and he would always find me. Next time, I would wait with closed eyes as he ran away and hid. And I would find him. He loved colored M&Ms as well as apples and carrots. I loved them, too, so we would share. When he turned two, I broke him myself – meaning I began to climb up on his back and ride him. Funny thing was no one else could ride him for he was still a wild stallion. Once a teenage boy whom I did not know climbed over the fence and tried. Well, Lucky just bucked him off then chased him back over the barbed wire fence! That made me smile when I heard about it. I liked that I was the only rider for this wonderful horse.

Each day I would hurry home from school, stand at the fence and whistle. Then Lucky would come barreling up, stopping on a dime just in front of me. I mostly rode bareback and knew how Indians must have felt before we invaded their lands. Once a large rattlesnake appeared and angrily shook its rattle, Lucky, frightened, reared up and as I was riding bareback, I slid off over his tail to the ground. Lucky galloped away at the speed of light, leaving me inches from the outraged and poisonous rattler. I was too angry to be afraid of the snake, and stood up shouting for Lucky. I felt the snake saw I was angrier than he was, so he slid off pretty quickly, disappearing into the sage brush.

Sometimes my grandfather would let me go to a nearby friend's pastures who had hundreds of wild acres and I could ride bareback for hours in the wide open spaces under the blue, blue sky. How can I convey that feeling of galloping bareback towards an endless horizon, flat yet infinite, with the warmth of a Texas sun beating down, and a fierce wind blowing in my hair? That never-ending Texas horizon, a blue sky that just wouldn't quit, left me with the profound feeling that anything is possible. You know what? I still have that feeling to this very day, that anything is possible!

❖ What activity gives you that special feeling that anything

   is possible?

The Rabbit Who Came Back Home

Ever since I can remember, I was always bringing small live animals home, mostly baby animals needing to be rescued: abandoned kittens, a bird with a broken wing, and others. The kittens were so tiny I had to take an eye dropper and feed them every few hours. They would grow up and before long, I would have to put up signs, *Free Kittens*, to find homes for them all. One day, I discovered a wounded mockingbird. I took two popsicle sticks and made a bandage for the broken wing to heal. The bird would flop around for a time until, after a while, he could stand. Then the day would come when I would take it outside, unwrap the bandage, throw the popsicle stick away, and hold up the bird and release it. Would he fly away? Or fall down? I held my breath and made a wish that the bird would fly free. The sun was so bright I couldn't see well when I held him up to the sky. I gently tossed him up and away, waiting to see what would happen. The little bird flapped his wings hard and then happily flew up and away. I felt a little sad but mostly happy that he was free and flying again. After all, a bird must fly, mustn't he?

One day I was walking near my home and feeling the sun on my back and face.

I almost stepped on a small furry beast on the ground. I knelt down and there he was: a small furry baby rabbit, all alone and very, very thin. I gently picked him up and took him home. I took an old shoebox and put a towel in it then laid him down. I ran upstairs to the bathroom and found the eye dropper and got some milk, adding water to dilute the milk. Babies shouldn't drink full strength milk, that's why I added some water to the milk. I sat down and picked up the small bunny rabbit whose eyes were closed. I put the eye dropper in its little mouth and began to squeeze the dropper so a little milk would go down his throat. I said out loud, "Please live, little rabbit." He drank the milk and that made me smile. If he could swallow the milk, he might live. Every few hours, I would get up and feed him more milk, a little at a time. Every day, I would rush home from school and feed him more milk. One day, his eyes opened wide and this made me very happy, for now I knew for certain that he would live.

I called him 'Peter Rabbit' from the stories written by Beatrix Potter from England. Peter was the sweetest little rabbit and so cuddly, too. Peter grew and grew and grew until before very long, he was hopping around. He would hop up in my lap and go to sleep there. We had such good times together. Before long, Peter was strong and had grown to be a young rabbit and no longer a weak, baby bunny. I felt a bit sad, but knew it was time to set him free.

After school, I walked home very slowly knowing what I had to do when I arrived home. As if waiting for me, I saw Peter Rabbit. I picked him up and hugged him and almost cried. Then I went outside and set him down on the grass and told him to go, go, go! You're strong now and must hop away. For a while, Peter was confused and just stayed there, not moving. Then I shooed him away and only then did he hop, hop, hop away.

The next day I felt sad, but after a few days I was better, especially thinking of Peter free and living a happy, rabbit life, perhaps meeting other rabbits like himself.

After three days, imagine my surprise, when I came home from school and saw Peter standing exactly where I had set him free. "Peter," I cried out, you have come back home!" From then on, for a very long while, Peter would come back home for a visit and I would have a carrot waiting for him to eat.

Then he would hop, hop, hop away back to freedom. I didn't mind, for I knew that another day, Peter Rabbit would come back home once again. I knew this because we were now good friends. Once good friends, always good friends – even if they sometimes hop away!

❖ Who are some of your good friends that sometimes hop away?

❖ Think of an animal or bird who became your good friend too.

The Tree House

When I was little but in school, whenever it was late afternoon near dinner time and my Mother or grandparents wondered where I was, you could bet I'd be up a tree somewhere. One of my favorite pastimes was taking a book then climbing a favorite tree. Then I would rest on the branches, look up at the sky at passing clouds, or at whatever was going on down below, or simply open my book and read and read. It was quiet, nobody was there to talk, and I could pass an hour just being by myself high up in the tree, in my own private world.

Well, Daddy Milt, who was my grandfather, noticed that I was always climbing trees. So, one sunny day, he asked if I'd like to build a tree house. Would I? You bet. So first we found some old boards no longer in use lying about behind the garage or wash house. Then I was told to pick out a tree. I took my time looking at all the trees on our property because I wanted to be sure and pick a good one for my tree house. Finally, I found a live oak tree fairly tall but not too old and not too high, still easy to climb up. "That's the one," I told my grandfather.

Then the work began. I would climb up halfway and Daddy Milt would hand me a board then another board and so it went. He taught me how to hammer, making sure the nail was straight so the boards would hold fast. First, we made a railing to be sure nobody would accidently fall. Then we made a floor.

The tree's own branches were the roof. After two long afternoons after school, the tree house was finally done.

We carried the tools back and put them in the wash house then I slipped into the kitchen and took some of my grandmother's homemade cookies – chocolate chip – and ran to my very first tree house. The first day I enjoyed just sitting and looking all around, noticing things I didn't usually notice. For instance, a neighbor's black cat was prowling nearby looking for field mice or a young starling was flying all around making noise, looking for his mother. Once a wild rabbit ran below. I saw him but he didn't see me as I was so high up. I felt like this was my secret castle and no one could come unless I gave them permission.

The next day, along with some cookies, I brought my comic books, usually *Casper the Friendly Ghost* or Classic comics like *The Tale of Two Cities*. The classic comics cost a nickel more than the regular comics, but my grandmother didn't know how to say 'no' to me so I got what I wanted, mostly.

The next day I brought an old pillow in case I wanted to nap and some paper and crayons in case I felt like drawing. Oh, yes, and some cookies, too, of course.

After a few days of reading, drawing, and looking around above at the clouds and birds, and below at rabbits, squirrels, and the neighbor's black cat, I just spent time doing nothing. You know what? It felt wonderful just to do absolutely nothing in a special place all my own. Later I told my grandmother that I felt it was important sometimes to do absolutely nothing, and she laughed then saw that I was serious. After a moment, she hugged me and said, "I think you are quite right. Sometimes it's important just to be."

❖ Now, what would your tree house look like?

❖ Can you draw it? What color is it?

❖ Where would it be? What kind of tree?

❖ What would you see from up there?

❖ What would you carry up to your tree house? (Don't forget the cookies!)

My Invisible Friend

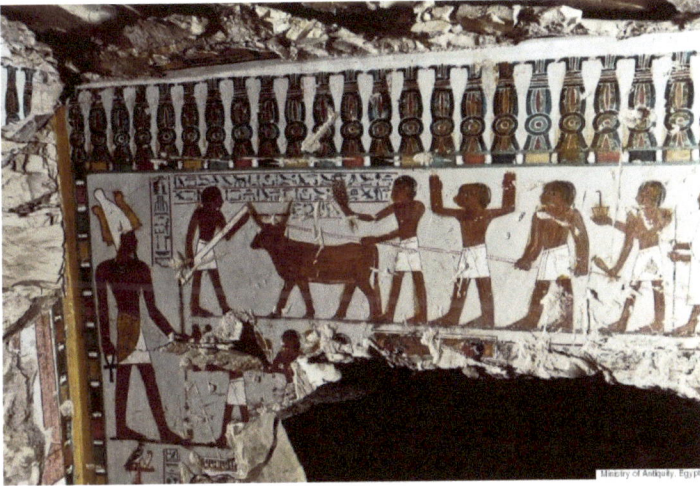

Ministry of Antiquity, Egypt

It was late at night, way passed my bedtime, and I lay in bed yet for some reason could not fall asleep. I was, as usual, alone in my upstairs bedroom, and no grown-ups were about. The wind was blowing and I heard the sound of the oak trees swishing this way and that, but I did not feel scared – not one little bit. I was seven years old and by now was quite use to sleeping alone in my room.

I yawned then turned over on my back and looked around, and that's when I first saw him. He was a tall man standing on the side at the foot of my bed. I don't know why but I was not afraid. Somehow, I knew he was there to protect me. He was a friend. Each night he would be there, standing quietly beside my bed. Though I clearly felt his good wishes for me, there were no words spoken. Words were not necessary.

I remember thinking how odd his clothes were, not the way people dress today. He wore a long white gown with blue and gold trim around the neck. Anyway, I became used to having him near me each night when I went to bed, and thought no more about it. That is, until, one afternoon, two weeks later.

There were no books to speak of in our house, other than the King James Bible, and several volumes of an encyclopedia called *The Book of Knowledge*. After reading the *Bible* all the way through twice, I would go to the hallway downstairs where the bookcase was, and lie down on the carpet and read from *The Book of Knowledge*. I began with Book A, then Book B, and so on. After sometime, I was reading Book E. I enjoyed reading these books as there were many fine pictures. One day I was reading about a place called Egypt and how people lived long, long ago. Imagine my surprise when I saw a drawing of 'my friend' standing by a large stone building, dressed in a white gown with blue and gold trim near his neck. This is when I knew that 'my friend' was from the Egypt of long, long ago. The book said he was a priest of some kind and was very, very wise. I was just happy that he came back to visit me.

Somehow, I knew not to talk about my friend with my family or friends or even teachers at school. Somehow, I knew they might not understand why I had a friend that no one else could see. I also knew that though 'my friend' was invisible to everyone else, he was, to me, very, very real.

❖ Can you think of a time you had a friend who was invisible to others but not to you?

❖ This friend can be a person or an animal or bird or tree or insect.

❖ Write about this 'invisible friend' and maybe draw a picture, too.

Chickens Are Stupid!

When I was little, my family moved to Texas. My father was away so my mother and I lived with her parents, my grandparents, Gram and Daddy Milt. My grandfather had retired so he didn't have to work anymore, but both he and Gram, my grandmother, had grown up on a farm in west Texas, and wanted to have a place with some farming so they bought several acres with a large, two-storied white house with ample land for animals and fields to grow vegetables. I always dreamed of having my own horse so later, Daddy Milt bought me a white mare called Babe – but that's another story.

Even though I was only seven years old, my grandparents thought I should have chores to teach me to be responsible or some such. So, I helped out on this little Texas farm. I actually loved being outdoors with my grandfather and helping him plant corn and hoe to dig in the soil and plant seeds for the vegetable garden. It's nice to feel useful, isn't it?

But there were certain chores I did not like at all – not even a little bit, and that was dealing with the chickens. They were noisy, always clucking and squawking. And they would sometimes pick on one of their own, pecking until the poor thing was hurt and bloody. They were not too bright even, all right, I'll say it, "Chickens are stupid." Why, they would eat anything. And the tiniest noise would send them into a panic of squawks and feathers flying. And unlike an outdoor cat who would be clean and thoughtful so you never had to clean up after a cat.

One of my chores after school was to clean the chicken bin, the

place where they lived inside a fence with little nests in a little

house. This was a dirty chore. Ugh!

The hen house was a little hut built of wood where the

hens – that is, the girl chickens – would sit on a little pile of hay

called a nest where they would lay eggs. I would daily collect

the eggs in a basket then carry them inside the house to the

kitchen, to my grandmother. Some evenings when we had a lot

of eggs, my grandmother and I would candle the eggs. We would

sit around the kitchen table with a little box with a light bulb in

it and place each egg into a hole in the box that would show us

what was inside the egg. This was a neat activity called *candling* and I actually enjoyed it. If we saw a little red blood inside, that egg would be set aside and not sold to the A & P which was the local grocery store that bought our eggs. Usually, I didn't mind collecting the eggs from the hens. Yet sometimes a hen would still be sitting on the eggs and my grandfather taught me how to reach under her and take the eggs. Well, that was simple enough only sometimes the stupid hen would peck me. And that could really hurt.

Cleaning out the chicken bin was the worst though. It made me cough because of the dirt and dust. And chickens are

not all that clean. They leave a big mess all over the place.

One thing though. Like a lot of folks, we never needed an alarm clock to wake us up every morning. Each and every morning at sunrise, the old rooster – that's the boy chicken - would crow loud and long. You'd think he thought if he didn't crow loudly enough, the sun wouldn't know when to rise.

Every so often, my grandfather and I would have to catch each chicken and clip their wings. This was so they wouldn't fly over the fence and get plum away.

What probably bothered me the most was that unlike a dog or a cat, chickens were not really pets. You couldn't stroke them or talk to them or ride them like a horse. They were just there and had to be taken care of, cleaned up after, and guarded so they wouldn't fly away. They were a chore, all right!

Every Easter, my grandparents would give me something special on Easter Sunday. It was always a surprise and always something 'live'. One year, a black lamb, another year, a white rabbit. Then one year, I awoke to find fifty colored baby chicks! They were blue and pink and green. I never saw such a thing. And I laughed, forgetting for the moment that these fifty soft and wiggling baby chicks would one day grow up to be

fifty stupid chickens.

After some time, I got use to the chickens and they got use to me, I guess, because when I would come and feed them, throwing out corn and such, they would gather around and not make such a fuss or squawk. In fact, they would cluck as if they were glad to see me. They even stop pecking me when I had to take the eggs from the nest. I also began watching them, studying them like. I noticed that the hens would take care of their chicks like any good mother would. They would teach them how to find little worms to eat or other bugs. (Of course, I wouldn't want my mother to do that! Who eats bugs! Ugh!)

I liked that they were a family, too, and that they took care of each other. Just like we do.

Guess when you take the time to look at creatures - or even people- long enough, you find things we all have in common.

❖ Think of a time you felt that a bird or animal was just like you.

❖ What was the bird or animal?

❖ Can you draw it?

The Magical Mimosa

When I was very young, I would spend a long, long time swinging on my swing near my house and just in front of a large mimosa tree with long, heavy, hanging branches. It was my custom to see how high the swing could possibly go without me falling out. I would aim to touch my big toe to one of the high branches of the mimosa tree. Of course, I knew I could never touch my big toe to the branch, but it gave me something to aim at.

An only child, I sometimes needed to talk with someone. So, after a time, while I was swinging higher and higher, I began to talk to the mimosa tree. The tree was a very kind tree, friendly, and would listen to me for the longest time, answering me by her flowering branches bobbing up and down, as if to say "Yes, yes, go on. Tell me more." This encouraged me to talk some more, tell her my problems at school that day or whatever. After we became friends, I would tell the tree my secret wishes – something I had never told anyone, ever. Once I told her that I wish I had a best friend who could come and play with me and have adventures. Well, you know what? Before long, I met Celia who was in my class at school and we liked all the same things. We even looked like sisters. Sometimes people would ask us if were sisters? And we liked that.

After this wish came true, I made a point to always tell the now magical mimosa tree all my wishes. I didn't think it was an accident that after telling her my wish for a best friend, that it actually happened!

Later on, I learned that there are friends everywhere. Not only human friends but animal friends and tree friends. Even stars and insect friends – even a butterfly friend. I also learned that magic is everywhere – even where you least expect it to be.

I am much older now and swing very rarely. Yet, even now, years and years later, whenever I see a mimosa tree anywhere, I will pause, say hello, and make a wish!

❖ What is a favorite place outdoors where you feel at home and can make a wish?

My Brother, David

I am an only child. This means I have no brothers or sisters. Just me. A funny thing happened the year we moved to Texas. I was seven years old then and, as I said, an only child. Except when at school, I had to play mostly by myself back at home. After a great deal of playing all by myself, I began to make a wish to the mimosa tree to have an older brother to play with. I would swing high in front of the great mimosa tree and tell my wish to the tree's blossoms. It was a magical mimosa so I figured there was a good chance that my wish would come true.

After wishing every day for some days, I came home from school one day and ran outside to play and there was David. He was a bit older, eight years old, and he said he was my brother. The Magical Mimosa Tree had sent him to me.

David and I got on tremendously. We liked to do the same adventures together like hiking across the fields, discovering new places, new insects or animals. We liked reading together outside under a tree. And we would talk and talk and talk, sometimes silly, silly talk and at other times, real serious talk.

I told the Magic Mimosa that I was so grateful that she sent David to me and how nice it was to have a big brother. David was very patient when I was late coming back from school some days. Yet he would never get angry or scold me like the grownups sometimes did.

All went well until one day just before dinner time, the

doorbell rang. It was a man who asked to speak to my mother. When she came, the man explained that he was from the school board and reading through the information forms filled out by the students, he was wondering why my brother, David, was not in school like his sister. My mother looked puzzled then annoyed and told the stranger that I was an only child and there was no brother called David or by any other name. That's when I got into trouble, big trouble.

I didn't tell them about my wishing for a big brother or about my telling the Magic Mimosa tree my wish or anything like that. Somehow, I just knew that they wouldn't believe me. Then the man asked me why I put down on the school form that I had an older brother named David. I told him, "Because that's his name. David."

Then my mother got really angry and said, "But he's not real. You made him up."

Then I got a little angry myself and said rather too loudly, "Well, he's real to me!"

The man almost smiled and excused himself, quickly leaving. Then my mother gave me that look that says "What am I going to do with you!" She then tried to explain to me the difference between what is real and what is made up. I just listened and didn't say much. There's so much grown-ups don't understand.

Then later that night, I climbed into bed and stayed awake thinking about David, about the man from the School Board, about my mother talking about what is real and what is made up. After a while, I felt sleepy and closed my eyes and you know what? There was David and he was smiling. Then just before I drifted off to sleep, I told myself, "What is real to me may not be real to other people. And that's OK."

❖ Did you ever make up someone or something that became real to you?

❖ Write or draw it.

The Cloud People

When I was very young, I would go outside and lie on the grass and watch the clouds drift by. The clouds were large and fluffy, always changing into one thing or another. I could lie on the grass for the longest time to watch all the magical creatures in the sky. I called them the 'cloud people' though, actually, not all were people. Some were animals or birds or even insects. I saw a giant duck once with a large open beak so big you could almost hear him quacking. Then I saw train tracks going on and on though I never saw a train. Once I saw a monkey with the longest tail and long hairy arms reaching out to catch the setting sun. Once he almost had the sun in his paws - but not quite. And his long tail kept twitching in excitement.

One time I saw three horses pulling a chariot across the sky. In olden times in Rome and Greece and India, men rode in chariots drawn by horses – hundreds of years before cars or even trains. They even rode and fought in chariots when they had great battles. Even way back, men were fighting over one thing or another.

Then suddenly the chariot was gone and the clouds

shifted, and in its place, I saw a great and powerful green dragon!

I called the dragon Mandrake for he was full of magic. I would close my eyes and dream that I was up in the sky riding on his back. But when I opened my eyes, would you believe it, Mandrake was gone, and something else was in his place. When you cloud watch, you have to keep an eye on whatever is there, because in the blink of an eye, it might change and you will never again see the same picture.

One day I saw a beautiful angel with wings.

Well, I guess you understand why I wanted to stay longer and longer lying on the grass, watching all the clouds pass by. I'm not sure that grown-ups realize how many wonderful things are happening right over their heads, up there in the sky, as they rarely look up at all. Even when it is time for dinner and my grandmother calls my name to come in to eat, I don't want to leave the cloud people. They're my friends. But I don't wish to upset my family so I promise the Cloud People that I will come again tomorrow and play with them. And I will, for sure!

❖ Now, what can you imagine seeing when you look up at the sky and the moving clouds?

❖ Write or draw it!

The Doll Collection

A fter fighting in two great wars, my father stayed on in the army, living in Europe, mostly, so I rarely saw him. He travelled a great deal and every birthday or Christmas would send me a special gift: a doll from some distant part of the world, from a place I had never been. So, after a few years, I had so many dolls, they needed a tall glass case to keep them all in. There were dolls from France, dolls from Switzerland, Sweden, Denmark, and Holland. Dolls from Italy and Greece. Dolls from Spain and Cuba. Dolls from everywhere! I already had dolls from Japan from when we – that is, my father and mother and I - all lived in Japan after the World War II. The two Japanese dolls were very tall and more to look at than to actually play with.

I would spend hours sitting on the floor, taking one or two of my dolls out from the glass cabinet then talking to them, and eventually I would make up a story of who they were, their names, and what it was like in France, Switzerland, Sweden, Norway, Denmark, Holland, Italy, Spain, Cuba, or Japan. As an only child - that means not having any brothers or sisters – as an only child, I had lots and lots of time by myself. So, these foreign dolls became my friends – friends from all over the world. That was pretty neat!

For instance, the tall, beautiful, standing doll from Japan, I called Princess Mineko after my Japanese nanny when we lived in Tokyo, Japan. I made her a princess as she was so beautiful. The doll was dressed as people were a long time ago in Japan, maybe as long ago as the Middle Ages. Princess Mineko wore a long silk orange kimono (a kind of dress) with sleeves even longer than her arms were, and with a black silk tilted hat on her head. She told me that even though she was a princess, she was a lonely princess as she, like me, was an only child, too. I told her I hoped to grow up to be as beautiful as she was. She liked that.

There was also a brother and sister doll from Holland. I called them Kim and Kana. They had blonde hair and funny cotton caps and were dressed as those who lived in the country where the weather is cold. And guess what? They had funny shoes made of wood. In Holland, they called them 'wooden clogs'. When they walked in their clogs, they went clop, clop, clop! That's funny, isn't it? Or maybe it's just different, that's all.

There was one little doll I grew very fond of from Switzerland. I called her Elizabeth. She wore white leather slippers, a bright green skirt with a white apron on top, a long sleeve white cotton blouse and a gray wool vest on top – for it got very cold up in the mountains in Switzerland. She also wore a woolen grey cap shaped like an upside-down ice cream cone with red and white flowers on it. Elizabeth had lovely yellow hair, beautiful, clear blue eyes, and a sweet red smile. Her face was white and delicate, maybe because in Switzerland they drink a lot of milk from their Swiss cows. Elizabeth was so tiny I could put her in my pocket and take her with me anywhere. Sometimes, too, I would let her sleep with me. I didn't have to put her back in the glass case like the other dolls who were much bigger. I guess you might say that she was my very special doll friend.

Then there was a doll from America but from long ago America. Her head was made of china so it was fragile and could break. I had to be very careful not to drop her on the floor. Her black hair was painted on as well as her eyes and mouth. The rest of her body was a white cotton print of red and blue and tan all stuffed with straw. She had arms with her hands painted onto the cloth dress. Unfortunately, she had no feet at all. I called her Evelyn – maybe because I had an Aunt Evelyn who I liked a lot. My Evelyn was a real lady, as well, so I would always be extra-polite when talking with her and ask her to sit and have tea or lemonade with me.

Later as I grew older, I would hear grown-ups say how sad it was that I was an only child and had no one to play with.

If they only knew how many I had to play with, if they only knew about my special friends from all over the world!

❖ There are all kinds of friends. Animals, butterflies, frogs, pretend friends, toys and dolls.

❖ What are some of your special friends?

RD   Thursday, November 14, 1957

Schedule Panorama Of Desi

--Kay Jones, ninth grade student at Bowie Junior High school, won first bby division at the State Fair of Texas with her collection of dolls from the dolls entered in the fair are but a part of Kay's collection. She is the rs. Dorothy Jones, 903 South Irving Heights Drive.--News Staff Photo.

Catherine, age 13, a first place Blue Ribbon for
The Doll Collection at the Texas State Fair.

Waiting

My father left us when I was four, and that made my mother very sad. I thought a lot about my father but rarely got to see him. Sometimes I felt like I was waiting for him to come home, but he never did.

However, I was blessed by a wonderful, wonderful

grandmother. My mother and I lived with her parents, my grandparents. My mother had to work as my father had to go away, so my grandparents took care of me. I called her Gram, and she was very, very special to me and I was to her. She would bake cookies and cobblers and cakes, then wait to put the crust in the oven so I could smell fresh crust baking as I came home from school. I would head straight to the kitchen as she would be taking out the crust from the oven just as I came in the door. Then she would take fresh butter and spread it on the hot crust so I could eat it. Gram knew that hot crust was a huge favorite with me. There would still be plenty of crust left over for the apple pie or peach cobbler - our after- dinner dessert!

I always loved going to the grocery store with Gram for after the shopping was done, she would let me pick out a new comic book then buy it for me. I especially liked the *Classic Comics* like *Tale of Two Cities* or *A Midsummer Night's Dream*. but they cost a little bit more. Somehow

Gram would buy them for me anyway, for she had trouble saying no to me, which was very nice.

Once we were in a large department store to buy clothes. I was never very interested in shopping for clothes but was told it was important for school and church so I went along. Walking down a large aisle, I spied some paintings, and one painting in particular, caught my eye. Well, I couldn't take my eyes off this painting of a little girl with large brown eyes, sitting in a chair. The painting was called '*Waiting*'. And you could see, plain as day, that the little girl was sad and was waiting for something or someone. I felt I was looking into a mirror and knew this little girl and everything she was feeling, too.

I told my grandmother that I wanted to take this painting of the little girl home with me. Well, it cost much more than a comic book. I told Gram that if she would buy this painting for me that I would give up comic books for as long as it took to pay for the painting.

Gram smiled and was rather impressed with my bargaining, and besides, I knew that she couldn't really say 'no' to me. So, the painting of the little girl waiting came home with us that very day. I hung the painting in my room and would spend a lot of time just gazing and gazing at the little girl and the title underneath which said, "Waiting." Sometimes tears would come into my eyes as I knew everything the little girl was feeling. I don't think a single day would go by when I wouldn't look at this painting and feel something deep inside.

Then one day which started out to be a day like any other day, one day something unexpected happened when I was staring at the painting. I felt sad and then suddenly I knew what the little girl was waiting for. She, like me, was waiting for her Daddy to come back home.

Sometimes even when there are people at home who love you very much and take good care of you, sometimes there is still something or someone missing.

❖ Sometimes there is something or someone that you, too, may be waiting for.

❖ What is something or someone you are waiting for?

Catherine, age 7

Learning Patience the Hard Way

Growing up, I was a tomboy. That means even though I was a girl, I played more with the boys and liked boy-kind of games and adventures. The boys always chose me for the football team as I was a good kicker. I would kick barefoot and knew just where to hit the ball and often this meant we would win the game. Sometimes everyone would tumble over everybody else and it was rough but fun.

I especially loved climbing trees and could climb higher and higher to the top of the tree. Wrestling was fun, too, and I would never give up when someone jumped and wrestled with me. Baseball was a favorite game in my neighborhood and I played first base and though I wasn't the best hitter when I came to bat, I did well enough to stay on the team.

Riding bicycles was also a favorite sport. My friends and I would ride and ride.

I would also ride to school every day, every school day, I mean. I had a red bicycle as red was my most favorite color. Sometimes I'd bike so fast it was like flying in the wind.

I named my red bike, Charger, and he never let me down. Sometimes I would ride in circles in our two-car garage. It helped me learn how to turn corners better. I would sing songs as I rode round and round and round. Then I did it long enough that I could go faster and faster and faster. I was singing "She'll be Comin' 'Round the Mountain" and going 'round and round and round when it happened.

My grandmother was always telling me to 'be patient' as she saw me always rushing about in a hurry. She had warned me not to go so fast but I didn't listen and just kept going faster and faster and faster. That is, until I crashed big time! At first, I wasn't sure what happened. One minute I was going round and round and round on Charger, singing "She'll be Comin' Round the Mountain" and the next I was lying on the garage floor and blood was everywhere. My little toe was barely hanging onto my foot. Blood all over the place. Of course, I was riding the bike, barefoot as I didn't like to wear shoes.

My grandmother at first thought I was playing a trick and

had used red paint to scare her. Sometimes I did play tricks but not this time. This was real. When she looked closer, she saw that I was in big trouble and brought a towel to wrap my foot then put me in the car. We drove lickily-split to Dr. Irving. And we didn't have to wait either. Dr. Irving was our family doctor. Everyone liked Dr. Irving. After cleaning the foot of all the blood, he warned me that he was going to sew my toe on so I wouldn't lose it. And that this might hurt. Well, there was no might about it. It did hurt – and how! But I bit my lip and kept thinking better to feel a little pain than lose my little toe forever. It didn't take all that long because Dr. Irving was a good doctor. Both Gram and I felt a whole lot better after it was all done.

On the way back home, Gram stopped at Baskin-Robbins and we had ice cream. Gram had strawberry and I had chocolate almond. She made me promise three things: 1) not to ride Charger, my bike, around the garage and 2) never to ride barefoot again. I promised both while licking my ice cream cone. Then I asked Gram what's the third promise? Gram stopped eating her ice cream cone, looked me square in the eyes, and said, "I want you to promise me to be more patient. You don't have to do everything so fast." Well, I promised because I knew Gram loved me and wanted me to be safe. But, the plain truth is, I'm still working on that third promise to this very day! Sometimes when too much in a hurry, you, too, might have to learn patience the hard way.

❖ What is something you have to be more patient with?

❖ Now practice doing it more slowly.

The First Time I Saw God

It was just after a great war where grown-ups were fighting each other for some years. It wasn't the first time either because they called this war, World War II, so it must have happened before. My father was in the army and was told to go and work in Japan, so my mother and I travelled on a great ship from America to Japan. My father had yet to meet me since before I was born, he was off somewhere in the Pacific fighting the Japanese. Now we were going to live in their country. My father said that we would live in Japan for two years. It was all a bit of a puzzle when you're too little to understand everything.

Mother and I were several days on a huge ship going to Japan. It was a great adventure. Once I got lost and thought the laundry chute was a slide to play on, and I climbed up and enjoyed going down the slide then falling into a pile of white sheets. I was told never to do that again, and I didn't. But it was fun! Soon after we arrived in Tokyo, I fell sick and had to be taken to a hospital. There they operated and removed my tonsils and I couldn't talk for a while. I remember most that I was given ice cream after the operation and that was very tasty.

We lived in a nice, airy house full of light, with five Japanese servants. Meneko was my nanny and I liked her a lot. From her, I quickly learned to speak Japanese and would translate between the servants and my parents. Children learn other languages much easier than grown-ups or so I was later told.

My father had a pet monkey who was very jealous if anyone came near my father. The monkey would screech loudly and try to bite me when I wanted to sit on my father's lap. Mean little monkey. I forget his name, probably because I didn't like him.

One Sunday afternoon, we went outside Tokyo to a tremendous park in a place called Kamakura. Cherry trees were in bloom and they smelled like honey. We saw bright pink flowers on the trees everywhere. We sat down and had a picnic. My mother told me years later that when I saw little children who looked hungry, I would give away our food to them. Then after lunch, we walked to a nearby temple. I didn't know then what a temple was but I think it is something like a church. Meneko, my nanny, wanted me to see something special and took me away. It was there in Kamakura near the temple that I first saw God.

At first, I thought it was a mountain. It was so big, giant. Yet when we got close, I looked up and there He was. I remember feeling very, very small and looking up at this beautiful man who was very, very big. His eyes were closed and his face seemed to be smiling. Meneko told me softly that this was Lord Buddha. I couldn't talk for some time but remember looking up at Him and thinking, "Oh, this is what they mean by God."

It was very peaceful there, and though I was only four, I never forgot Him. Ever since that day, I always felt that there was something far greater than human beings. I also felt protected by this something far greater than I was. It was this feeling that stayed with me though the picture of what God is changed as I grew up. Later I understood that God wasn't a bronze statue or a painting of some religious deity or god, but it was that deep, deep feeling inside that there is something far greater than man, and it is always there looking over us. Once you know this, it doesn't really matter what God looks like. He may look different to different people, people all over this world.

It's more than enough to know this Presence is there, and that it

never, never goes away.

❖ What does God look like to you?

❖ Can you draw it?

About the Author

Catherine Ann Jones** is an award-winning author (*Heal Your Self with Writing, Buddha & the Dancing Girl*), playwright (*Calamity Jane, On the Edge*), and screenwriter *(Touched by an Angel* series; *Unlikely Angel* with Dolly Parton)*, a professor, and Fulbright scholar. She offers writing workshops in the U.S. and abroad, writing consultations, and over 56,000 subscribers to her online courses. A mother and grandmother, she has one son and now two grandsons. **www.wayofstory.com**

www.ingramcontent.com/pod-product-compliance
Lightning Source LLC
Chambersburg PA
CBHW042042090426
42733CB00027B/50